Bears

Written by

Teresa Brand and Natalie Bacich

World Teachers Press®

Published with the permission of R.I.C. Publications Pty. Ltd.

Copyright © 1999 by Didax, Inc., Rowley, MA 01969. All rights reserved.

First published by R.I.C. Publications Pty. Ltd., Perth, Western Australia.

Printed in the United States of America.

Order Number 2-5078
ISBN 1-58324-000-4

A B C D E F 99 00 01 02

Educational Resources

395 Main Street
Rowley, MA 01969

Foreword

The activities in this book recognize that speaking, listening, reading, writing and spelling are critical communication skills and development in any one of these skills is linked to development in the others. Consequently, the main teaching elements of language are covered at least once per week. The activities can be followed as a series of whole class activities or the class can be divided into five groups, so that in a week the groups rotate daily through the five activities. This particular strategy is successful when an adult leader is assigned to each group. These group leaders can include teacher assistants, parent helpers, or student teachers.

The activities enable you to respond to identified needs and provide relevant strategies to improve learning outcomes for students in their development as independent learners.

Simple directions for each activity sheet are found on pages 4 to 7.

Contents

Week Two

Activity Number	Week Two Strategy	Lesson Procedure
1 page 13	**Spelling** — letter sounds	**Sound – "Bb"** · Teacher reads *The Three Bears* story. · Make a list of all "Bb" words in story on chalkboard. · Children color the pictures on worksheet, circling each "b" letter. · Cut along the dotted lines and make into a little "Bb" book. Read to a partner.
2 page 14	**Spelling** — word study	**Word Sort** · Have words from worksheet on flashcards. · Read and emphasize final sounds "d," "l" and "r." · Children work together to sort into groups. · Children cut along the dotted lines and paste on the worksheet.
3 page 15	**Oral Language** — literacy-related skills	**Circle Story** · Discuss and review *The Three Bears* story with the children, in groups of eight. · Give each child a part and sit in a circle in correct sequence. · Children complete each sentence to re-tell the story. · As a conclusion, children can draw their part.
4 page 16	**Writing** — teaching children how to write informational text	**Recipe Procedure** · Read the recipe procedure to the group. · Children measure what is needed. · Follow "What to do" steps. · Teacher writes children's concluding statements onto strips. Children copy onto their sheets.
5 page 17	**Reading** — reading comprehension	**Change the Form - Picture Book** · As a group, determine the main events of the *The Three Bears* story. · Children working individually or in pairs, choose an event to illustrate. · Give children the matching strip to keep a track of who is illustrating each event. · Put pictures in order and staple together to make a book. Depending on how many children are in

Week One

Activity Number	Week One Strategy	Lesson Procedure
1 page 8	**Reading** — reading comprehension	**Reflection Session** · After reading any version of *The Three Bears*, teacher models questions that require children to think about the text; e.g., 1. What is the title? 2. Who are the characters? · After reflecting, children make their own little book to color and read to a partner/teacher.
2 page 9	**Reading** — reading comprehension	**Sentence Matching** · Teacher writes sentences from the worksheet on the chalkboard. · Children practice reading the sentences. · Children cut out sentences and glue in correct order.
3 page 10	**Oral Language** — literacy-related skills	**Story Reconstruction** · Retell the story as a group. · Children then color, cut, sequence and glue the pictures in sequence.
4 page 11	**Spelling** — word study	**Closed Word Sort** · Teacher puts a large "b," "h" and "s" on the chalkboard. · Teacher reads the *The Three Bears* story. · Words beginning with "b," "h" and "s" from the story are listed on chalkboard. · Children complete worksheet.
5 page 12	**Reading** — reading comprehension	**Sight Words in Context** · Introduce or review "yes," "no," "I," "can" and "see." · Ask children who they can see at the top of the worksheet. · Read through sheet with children. · Children complete worksheet by coloring "yes" or "no" and finishing pictures. · Children copy sentences.

Week Four Strategy

Activity Number	Strategy	Lesson Procedure
1 (page 23)	**Reading** — reading comprehension	**Brainstorm** • Ask children to orally retell *The Three Bears*. • Discuss/explain terms "setting," "characters," "events" and "themes." • Complete story worksheet box by box, coloring or drawing pictures.
2 (page 24)	**Reading** — reading comprehension	**Character Self-Portrait** • Teacher models a self-portrait of Father Bear using children's ideas. • Children complete their own self-portrait of him by writing.
3 (page 25)	**Spelling** — word study	**Word Sort** • Using "st," "sp" and "sl" teacher models lists on board using children's ideas. • Children complete their own word sort of "st," "sp" and "sl" words.
4 (page 26)	**Spelling** — phonics	**Sound Sleuth – "th"** • Teacher prints sentences on board. "Once upon a time there were three bears, Father Bear, Mother Bear, and Baby Bear." • Children help identify and circle all "th" words. • Children complete worksheets.
5 (page 27)	**Oral Language** — literacy-related skills	**Character Role-Play** • *Goldilocks and The Three Bears* masks—children choose one to wear. • Children color and complete masks. • Cut out mask and attach a band or elastic/ribbon with staples. • When masks are complete, children combine in groups to act out the story.

Week Three Strategy

Activity Number	Strategy	Lesson Procedure
1 (page 18)	**Oral Language** — language of social interaction	**Story Cloze** • As a group, discuss what the characters are saying in the cartoon about *The Three Bears*. • Children then complete their own with or without teacher help.
2 (page 19)	**Reading** — reading comprehension	**Character Self-Portrait** • Teacher models a self-portrait of Goldilocks using children's ideas. • Children complete their own self-portrait of Goldilocks by writing.
3 (page 20)	**Spelling** — phonics	**Building Words** • Teacher models some of the words by making a list of "er" words on the chalkboard. • Children then make their own "er" words on the worksheet and draw pictures.
4 (page 21)	**Reading** — reading comprehension	**Jumbled Story** • Teacher reads sentences with children. • Children cut and reassemble the story, correctly numbering each sentence. • Sentence strips can be glued in correct order on a large sheet of paper.
5 (page 22)	**Oral Language** — literacy-related skills	**Grid** • Teacher introduces children to the grid. • Children take turns describing positions of objects for others to locate. • Children complete worksheet. • Alternatively, children can describe the object, e.g., It has four legs and you sit on it. Answer: (4,C)

Week Six

Activity Number	Week Six Strategy	Lesson Procedure
1 page 33	**Writing** — teaching children how to write informational text	**Recount** • Teacher begins recording children's ideas of events of the Teddy Bears' Picnic. • Teacher models writing a story of the picnic. • Children complete their own story with words and pictures.
2 page 34	**Reading** — reading comprehension	**Wanted Poster** • Children draw in their own teddy. • Children complete "Wanted" poster by writing in details. • Children share posters, compare and contrast teddies.
3 page 35	**Spelling** — phonics	**Letter Mobile** • Children color initial "b" and "c" sounds. • Children cut out and sort words. • Children glue words on streamers hanging below letters. • Children can draw pictures of words inside large letters.
4 page 36	**Oral Language** — literacy-related skills	**Teddy's Tea Party** • Children predict what might happen at the Teddy Bears' tea party. • Teacher reads drawing instructions. • Children compare/contrast pictures with a partner.
5 page 37	**Reading** — reading: experimental phase	**Reading Old Favorites** • Read together "Teddy Bear, Teddy Bear, turn around." • Children point to words. Focus on sight words. • Children draw their own bear. • Cut and assemble to make a book.

Week Five

Activity Number	Week Five Strategy	Lesson Procedure
1 page 28	**Oral Language/Reading** — language and thinking: early reading phase	**Linking to Writing** • Brainstorm different kinds of bears and their distinguishing features/characteristics. • Play an oral game of "What bear am I?" Teacher models and children take turns. • Read and complete "My Bear Book."
2 page 29	**Spelling** — word study	**Word Search** • Read/decode words that children are required to find. • Model and teach children how to find words using initial letter clues. • Children color pictures and/or check off words when they find them in the search.
3 page 30	**Oral Language** — language and thinking	**Comparison and Partner Activity** • Children "Draw the Bear," and check off boxes as they draw features. • After they have completed features they work with a partner to orally compare their bears. • Partners share findings with whole class or group.
4 page 31	**Spelling** — word study	**Rhyming Word Sort** • Brainstorm rhyming words for "fat" and "fair." • Children cut, sort and glue words under correct rhyming word.
5 page 32	**Writing** — teaching children how to write informational text	**Procedure** • Discuss Teddy Bears' Picnic to be held next week (or sometime in the near future). • Teacher models writing a procedure by brainstorming on blackboard with children the things that will be needed, etc. • Children complete worksheet with or without teacher help. • Children illustrate items needed on rug.

Week Eight Strategy

Activity Number	Strategy	Lesson Procedure
1 (page 43)	**Oral Language** — language and thinking	**Questioning and Logic** • This game is an adaptation of "20 Questions." • Teacher chooses a sentence and models asking appropriate questions to find out what sort of bear he/she is. • Discuss types of questions children can ask. • Play game with children. Evaluate questioning.
2 (page 44)	**Spelling** — word study	**Little Words in Big Words** • Teacher models finding little words in big words. e.g., **he** in **here**. • Children then complete worksheet by cutting, gluing and sorting words. Discuss which word has the most/least little words in it. • Children illustrate/color pictures to finish worksheet.
3 (page 45)	**Writing** — teaching children how to write informational text	**Report: A Bear** • Using the worksheet children complete a report on any bear they choose. • Share children's reports. • Children illustrate their chosen bear on the back of the worksheet.
4 (page 46)	**Oral Language** — language and thinking	**Semantic Grid** • Discuss differences between types of bears. • Children then complete worksheet in pairs/small groups by writing or drawing answers. • Encourage children to discuss their choices.
5 (page 47)	**Reading** — early reading phase	**Developing Sight Words** • Teacher models reading "My Book of Bear Truths." • Discuss each statement. • Children read and color answers (children can work in pairs). • Orally read text. • Cut and assemble to make a book.

Week Seven Strategy

Activity Number	Strategy	Lesson Procedure
1 (page 38)	**Oral Language** — literacy-related skills	**Making a Block Bear** • Teacher models making a bear out of blocks as pictured on worksheet (using pattern blocks). • Each child constructs own bear. • Show bear to partner and describe how they made it.
2 (page 39)	**Writing** — teaching children to write informational text	**Report** • Discuss function of reports. • Teacher models reading and writing report. • Children complete report worksheet. • Share reports with class or group.
3 (page 40)	**Reading** — reading comprehension	**Story Grammar** • Ask children "What can bears do?" • Record all responses on board. • Children use these responses to make their little story book "A bear can...." • Children draw pictures to show what bears can do.
4 (page 41)	**Reading** — reading comprehension	**Story Map** • Discuss The Three Bears' house as drawn on worksheet. • Teacher then models worksheet discussing reasons why Goldilocks moved around the house in the order she did. • Children map their own path drawing Goldilocks' footprints and gluing labels.
5 (page 42)	**Spelling** — phonetic phase	**Looking for Visual Patterns** • Brainstorm known "ee" words. e.g., see, green. • Teacher adds words to list. • Read through worksheet "ee" words. • Children find where words belong and glue them next to correct place.

My Book About "The Three Bears"

This is Mother Bear.
Mother Bear is big too.

I can read these words.

bears	is	the
Father	big	three
	this	Bear
	small	Goldilocks
		Mother
		Baby
		pretty

This is Father Bear.
Father Bear is big.

This is Goldilocks.
Goldilocks is pretty.

The Three Bears

Name: _____

This is Baby Bear.
Baby Bear is small.

Sentence Matching

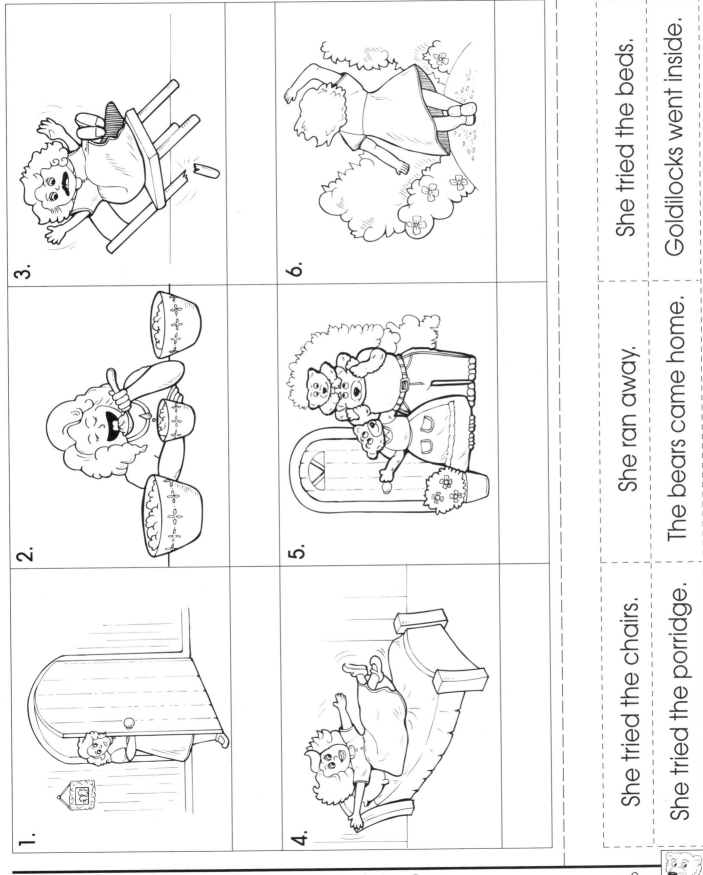

She tried the beds.

Goldilocks went inside.

She ran away.

The bears came home.

She tried the chairs.

She tried the porridge.

"The Three Bears"

Word Sort

b	h	s

hot	stand	hard
bear	high	sit
small	baby	bed
house	sob	sleep
big	bowl	hungry

Who Can You See?

I can see Father Bear. | yes | no |

_____ _____ _____ _____

I can see their house. | yes | no |

_____ _____ _____ _____

I can see Goldilocks. | yes | no |

_____ _____ _____ _____

I can see Mother Bear. | yes | no |

_____ _____ _____ _____

I can see Baby Bear. | yes | no |

_____ _____ _____ _____

My "Bb" Book

Name: _____

bear

bed

bowl

bow

broken

big

baby

Word Sort – Final Sounds

d	l	r

bowl

bed

growl

bear

girl

chair

said

door

head

Circle Story

1st — Once upon a time…

2nd — One morning Mother Bear made some porridge…

3rd — While the bears were out walking…

4th — Goldilocks tried Father Bear's porridge…

5th — Goldilocks sat in Father Bear's chair…

6th — Goldilocks went upstairs…

7th — When the bears came home…

8th — When Goldilocks saw the bears she…

How to Make Porridge

Porridge

What we need:

1 cup of oats   honey

2 cups of water   sugar   milk

What to do:

1. Mix the oats and water in the saucepan.

2. Put the saucepan on the stove and stir.

3. Bring the oats and water to a boil.

4. Put honey, sugar, or milk on top.

5. Share and eat.

What did the porridge taste like? _____

_____

_____

_____

Picture Book

The porridge was hot.

The bears went for a walk.

Goldilocks went to the bears' house.

She ate the porridge.

She sat on the chairs.

She broke Baby Bear's chair.

She laid on the beds.

She fell asleep in Baby Bear's bed.

The bears came home.

Goldilocks ran away.

"The Three Bears" –Cartoon

World Teachers Press® Blackline Masters – Early Theme Series – Bears

All About Goldilocks
Goldilocks

I am: _____

I live: _____

I eat: _____

I like: _____

I dislike: _____

I wish: _____

Building Words

riv

small   sist

moth —— **er**   fath

h   tall
broth

mother

I made ⬚ words.

Jumbled Story

Goldilocks ran away.

Goldilocks went to sleep.

The bears went for a walk.

Goldilocks sat in the chair.

Goldilocks ate the porridge.

1

Bear Grid

Can you find?

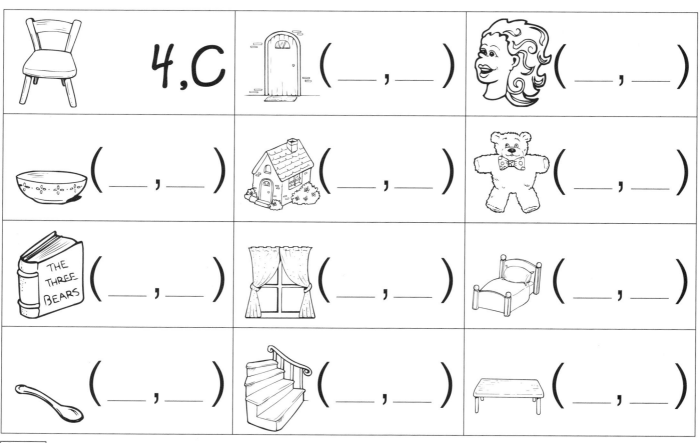

"The Three Bears"

Theme

Don't break into other people's houses.

The Characters

Father Bear

Mother Bear

Baby Bear

Goldilocks

Setting

The woods

The house

Events

1.

2.

3.

4.

5.

All About Father Bear

Father Bear

I am: _____

I live: _____

I eat: _____

I like: _____

I dislike: _____

I wish: _____

World Teachers Press® Blackline Masters – Early Theme Series – Bears

Word Sort

st	sp	sl

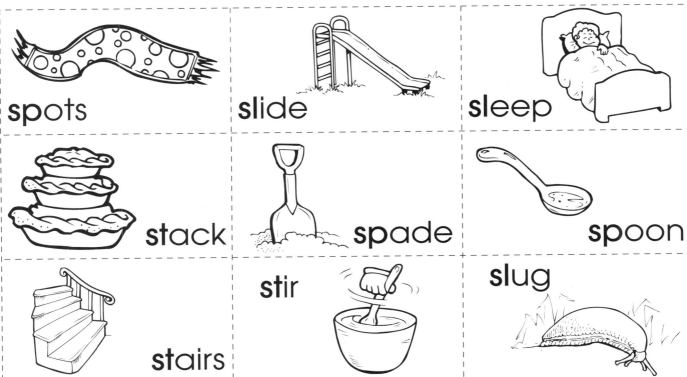

spots

slide

sleep

stack

spade

spoon

stairs

stir

slug

Missing Sounds

Once upon a time _____ere were _____ree bears,

Fa_____er Bear, Mo_____er Bear and Baby Bear.

Draw the three bears.

_____is is Mo_____er Bear.

_____is is Fa_____er Bear.

_____is is Baby Bear.

 World Teachers Press® Blackline Masters – Early Theme Series – Bears

Goldilocks and the Three Bears

My Bear Book

by _____

I am black and white.
My eyes are
black.
My tummy
is white.

I am a _____ bear.

I am not a bear.
I live in Australia.
I eat gum leaves.

I am a _____ .

I am a toy.
I like cuddles.
I like picnics.

I am a _____ bear.

I am white.
I live on the ice
and in the snow.

I am a _____ bear.

I am brown.
I am very big.
I like honey.

I am a _____ bear.

I am a baby bear.
I stay with my mum.

I am a bear _____ .

I can write these words.

cub

polar

koala

panda

grizzly

teddy

Word Search

big  small  honey

cub  panda  bear

hot  cold  baby

the   and   that

t	h	a	t	b	i	g	p
a	h	l	s	b	o	b	a
t	o	c	m	c	i	e	n
h	n	u	a	o	a	a	d
e	e	b	l	l	n	r	a
t	y	d	l	d	d	y	r
h	o	t	h	b	a	b	y

Draw the Bear

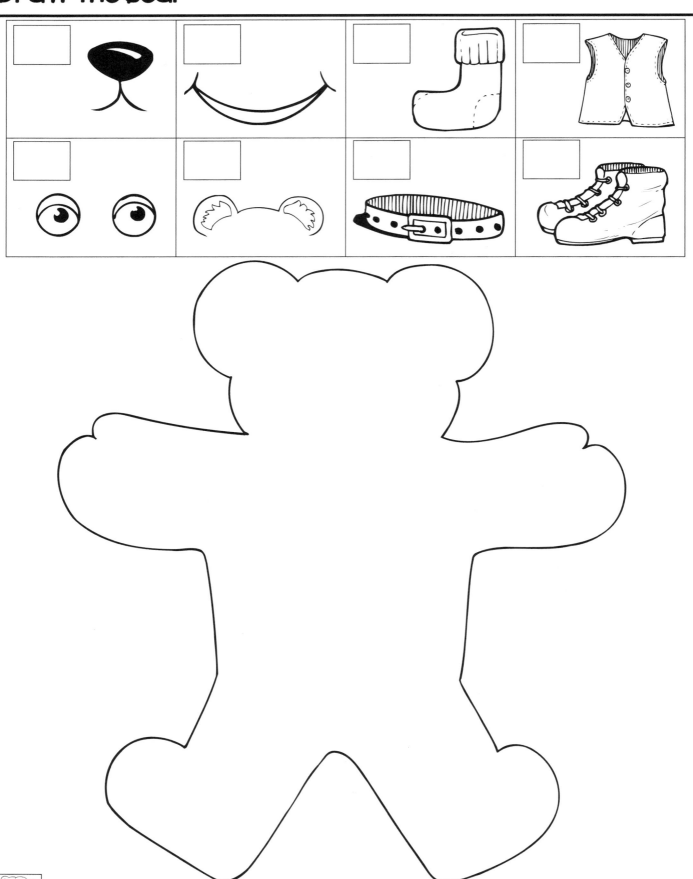

World Teachers Press® Blackline Masters – Early Theme Series – Bears

Rhyming Words

words that rhyme with **"fair"**

words that rhyme with **"fat"**

stair

hair

hat

bat

chair

pear

bear

rat

cat

mat

Our Teddy Bears' Picnic

Things we need...

_____

_____

_____

_____

_____

Things we do...

_____

_____

_____

_____

All About Our Picnic

On _____ we had our
Teddy Bears' Picnic.

Name: _____

Age: _____

Color: _____

Height: _____

Last seen at _____ house.

Make a Letter Mobile

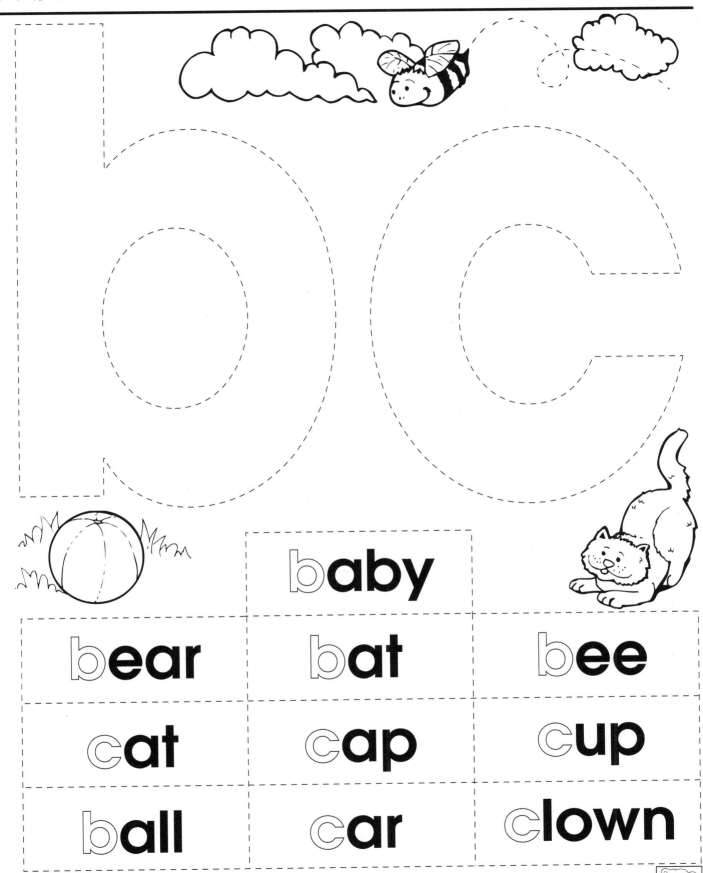

baby

bear

bat

bee

cat

cap

cup

ball

car

clown

Teddy's Tea Party

1. Take out your black crayon.

2. Draw the ground.

3. Draw a sun in the sky.

4. Draw your teddy standing on the ground.

5. Draw your favorite friend next to teddy.

6. Draw a table on the ground.

7. Teddy is having a tea party. Draw some things on the table.

Teddy Bear

by _____ 1.

Teddy Bear,
Teddy Bear
turn around.

2.

Teddy Bear,
Teddy Bear
touch the
ground.

3.

Teddy Bear,
Teddy Bear
tie your
shoe.

4.

Teddy Bear,
Teddy Bear
that will do.

5.

Teddy Bear,
Teddy Bear
go upstairs.

6.

Teddy Bear,
Teddy Bear
say your
prayers.

7.

Teddy Bear,
Teddy Bear
switch off
the light.

8.

Teddy Bear,
Teddy Bear
say,
"Goodnight!"

9.

Draw your teddy.

10.

Making a Block Bear

This is how I made a bear out of blocks.

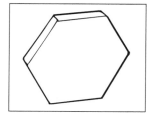 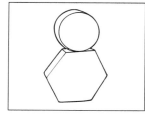 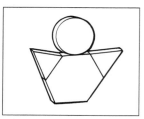 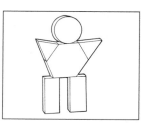

My block bear is yellow and blue. It is pretty.

Draw how you made a block bear.

1.	2.
3.	4.

Write a story about your block bear.

_____

_____

_____

World Teachers Press® Blackline Masters – Early Theme Series – Bears

All About My Teddy

My Teddy

My teddy has _____ fur.

My teddy has _____ legs.

My teddy has _____ arms.

My teddy has _____ eyes.

My teddy is _____ years old.

This is where my teddy lives.	This is what my teddy likes to do.

I like my teddy because _____

_____

_____.

A Bear Can...

by: _____

A bear can _____.

A bear can _____.

A bear can _____.

A bear can _____.

A bear can _____.

A bear can _____.

A bear can _____.

World Teachers Press® Blackline Masters – Early Theme Series – Bears

Story Map

| door | stairs | light | beds | mat |

Where Do the "ee" Words Go?

green	tree	feet	three
bee	queen	weep	see

World Teachers Press® Blackline Masters – Early Theme Series – Bears

I am a Polar Bear.

I am a Grizzly Bear.

I am a Panda.

I am a Bear Cub.

I am a Teddy Bear.

Little Words in Big Words

Can you find little words in these big words?

panda	bear	bamboo	forest

Draw a panda. Color the bear. Draw some bamboo. Color the forest.

rest	ear	for	and	or	ore
pan	am	be	boo	a a	a an
				a	a

My Bear Report

I am a _____ bear.

I have _____ fur.

I live in _____.

I like to _____

_____.

I can _____

_____.

I am a very special bear because _____

_____.

Draw your bear on the back of this sheet.

Bear Grid

	Panda Bear	Polar Bear	Grizzly Bear
Color of fur			
Where they live			
Favorite food			
Unusual features			
Color how they look			

Use these clues to help you to fill in the grid.

- black and white
- brown
- America
- China
- white
- seals
- Arctic
- bamboo
- honey

World Teachers Press® Blackline Masters – Early Theme Series – Bears

My Book of Bear Truths

by _____

If I was a Polar Bear, I would hunt for seals.

| True | False |

If I was a Panda Bear, I would swim.

| True | False |

If I was a Grizzly Bear, I would growl to protect my cubs.

| True | False |

If I was a Bear Cub, I could run fast.

| True | False |

If I was a Teddy Bear, I would like picnics.

| True | False |

I am a Koala and I am not a bear.

| True | False |

I can read these words.

not   I   and

                    like   if

          a   in

live   was   am

          to

for   have   my